MW01235140

RETURN
TO CENTER,
THAT ADDRESS
NOW KNOWN

RETURN TO CENTER, THAT ADDRESS NOW KNOWN

✳

A Little Guide
Toward Evolution
In The Light

LAURA CRUGER

AWAKE!™
INCORPORATED

Richmond, Virginia

FIRST PRINTING, OCTOBER 1994

ISBN 0-9643566-0-0
Printed in the
U.S.A.

DEDICATION

To All.
To All Teachers,
All Friends, To All My Relations.
To You, in Your Becoming.

IDEAS
ON HOW TO
USE THIS BOOK

Read it.

*Read between the
lines and DO the things in it.*

*DO any good thing that occurs
to you before, during or after reading.*

*Use it as an oracle by opening a page at
random, reading it, and applying what it says.*

*Or go through the chapters methodically,
using each one as a STEP deeper into the Center.*

*Write down your favorite parts of it or inspiring
things you make up while reading it, and tape
them to the wall or the refrigerator or your
dashboard or your toothbrush.*

*Disregard anything
that doesn't feel right for you.*

*Embrace and play with anything that
does, figuring out creative ways
to incorporate that thing
into your life.*

*Find your own
creative ways of SHARING
what you have been reminded of.*

CONTENTS

⑥

PART ONE

PART TWO

AFTER WORDS

PART ONE

The Center Place
(inspired by Dan Millman)

I go into that Center Place,
and stay awhile, and then I play
among the many strewn aside and
wandering astray.

I'll always trust that Center Place,
where silence Crisp lights past the fray

though in my mortal fainting mind I may forget

so please remind me that there is a Center Place,
and that I know the Way.

JUST SAY
NO
TO MENTAL
SELF-TORMENT

IDEAS
FOR ENDING
MENTAL SELF-TORMENT

Pay attention to
your inner dialogue.
Notice it the next time you
criticize yourself in your mind.
Can you detect its original source?
Whose critical voice is it?
Can you dodge it?
Can you heal it?

Write down all the things
about yourself that bug you.
What is true and changeable?
What on your list is a lie?

Daydream about
what it would be like
if you thought only nice
things about yourself.

Figure out how to become really really quiet.
Deep quiet. Quieter on the Inside
than You've Ever Been Before.
How does this feel?

THAT'S RIGHT, JUST SAY NO.

What is mental self-torment, anyway? you may be asking. It is the state of mind into which many of us fall when we beat up on ourselves with our own thoughts.

Sometimes, we are not fully aware that we do this; we just experience an underlying, pervasive sense of mild grief, despair or depression on a fairly regular basis, but can't quite put our finger on the source.

Haven't you experienced this? That nagging sense that something is just not right?

Do you remember when your mom yelled at you for not picking up your toys? Or perhaps you had a teacher who never looked you directly in the eye, never patted your back and said kind words to you. These things cut us to the quick; they fool our developing, innocent child-minds into thinking we are not good enough, that we are not the Wonderful Beings we once knew we were.

After we heard these scoldings for long enough and had to do without the attention we needed, we began to repeat unkind words to ourselves in our own minds. Our delicate neural pathways became frequent hosts to all manner of unniceties that we aimed at our very own innocent little selves.

Deep down inside we know this criticism is unfair and untrue and has no basis in reality. We may try to pretend we are not criticizing ourselves (*i.e.*, denial). Or we may give up the fight and even fall into patterns of speaking about how bad we are to others (*i.e.*, lying).

At this stage, any comfort we can get—any way we can momentarily forget these unpleasant thoughts, and steal a second of seeming inner peace or non-remembrance of these "bad things" about ourselves—seems like a good idea. This is when many of us fall prey to addictive behavior, which at first offers a release, a hiding, from how terrible we usually feel.

The problem is, the addictive act does not satisfy and soothe forever. In many cases, our bodies get used to whatever we are using, and the original pleasurable effect no longer occurs. But in an effort to re-experience that original feeling of peace and relief, we become compulsive and often can't stop doing this activity. It is no longer pleasurable, and the fact that we "do it anyway" becomes another addition to the arsenal of negative comments we can make about ourselves and about how our lives are going.

You see, addiction in any form is more about mental self-torment than it is about a desire to commit the beloved addictive act. In fact, we may even be able to label mental self-torment a form of addiction.

Let's redefine addiction.

An addiction is Anything We Do That We Don't Really Want To Do. It is anything that lessens the quality of our life. It may even be *not* doing something we really want to do. And it is anything that, after we've done it, we feel bad about it and wish we hadn't. Yet somehow we feel compelled...compelled to eat that chocolate chip cookie, compelled to work and work beyond the state of exhaustion, compelled to stay in bed when it only makes us feel more tired, compelled—on a more obvious note—to drink to excess, or to use cocaine or other addictive drugs. Sometimes, a part of our brain thinks we want to do the addictive act because it is attempting to give us pleasure. But the real us knows that doing it is bad for us. Therefore, we have an inner conflict and may even have arguments with ourselves.

Often, the performance of the act is merely a result of this mental battle and wrong thinking. We sigh—defeated again.

There is, believe it or not, a bright side to all of this: if the cause of the addiction is wrong-thinking, then it follows, fairly reasonably, that if we change our thinking, we can change our behavior, no?

The Act of the addiction becomes Unimportant when one is not Tormenting oneself about it! The Result of the act is ultimately physical or mental pain. Once we clear away the destructive thinking that leads to repetition of the act, we can easily choose not to inflict pain on ourselves.

We now see that the root of bad habits is Wrong Thinking!

*Yes, well...*you may be saying. *It's just not that easy. It's hard to overcome my bad habits...*

SO IT'S HARD OVERCOMING BAD HABITS.

DO IT ANYWAY.

UNUSUAL IDEAS
FOR OVERCOMING
BAD HABITS

Watch a sunset.
Notice how it begins,
endures, and ends.

Take five minutes in the
middle of the day to relax,
close the eyes, and do nothing.

Next time you get a little cut,
notice how it heals in a few days.

Next time you are tempted
to indulge in a habit, decide not to do it—
just this once. Take a deep breath, and mentally
scan your body. Notice if you are tightening any
muscles, or if you are holding your breath.
What do you feel? Where do you feel it?
Try loosening your hold on the muscles. Allow yourself
to breathe. Allow yourself to be intuitive about why
you may have decided to hide this feeling. Would
acknowledging this feeling potentially lead to conflict?
Breathe deeper. ***Is there a new truth you can see***
about this situation that will serve you in your
healing? *You may find you no longer desire*
to act out the addictive behavior. You may
even find you have learned something.

THE WORLD AS WE KNOW IT IS A TEMPORARY STATE OF AFFAIRS. Being attached to anything temporary—including our bad habits and addictions—can only lead us deeper into one place: misery! Though our true Self is not temporary, the world and everything in it is.

Running from fix to fix can only lead to a worn out body and a constant feeling of failure.

It *is* possible to overcome unwanted habits! It is possible to get more tired of the pain a habit causes than we are soothed by indulging in the habit. At this point, we can finally do something about it.

We may make headway and overcome a habit, like compulsive overeating, for a while, only to slip back into the debilitating pattern again. We then feel a sense of failure— as if we must be the terrible person the world told us we were after all.

But I say, Don't Give Up! If you slip, get up and move along. Forgive yourself. Refuse to feel guilty. Pray harder. Or if the word "pray" bugs you, concentrate harder. Use the slip to your advantage: Become More Determined. Imagine an Invincible You, and ask this Invincible You to kindly remove the habit from your neural net.

I spent years being so tired of overeating that I literally prayed and prayed and prayed that this habit be removed from me. It would lose its hold, only to resurface during particularly stressful times. I could see the pattern after a long ride on this not-so-merry-go-round, and eventually began to have more conscious control over my eating habits. I read every book I could get my hands on, listened to tapes, concentrated harder, took deep breaths before eating, asked myself if there were something I was avoiding feeling or if my body actually needed food, and prayed some more.

Nowadays, I sometimes even forget to eat. Me? Forget to eat? Forget to eat *food?* It's true. If I was able to overcome this pattern of self-torment that had been with me for a seemingly endless eternity of pure you-know-what, I believe anyone can overcome any habit.

Here's to your ability to overcome any habit you wish to end! We can heal ourselves, and we can continue to regain our freedom and our peace of mind. It just takes a certain persistence, a tenacity.

Each of us has every ingredient for healing within. When we quiet our minds and bodies long enough to look within, we will see the truth of our own unique Power of Transformation.

The really fun part is, the more we pay attention and tune in to ourselves, the more we will find ourselves drawn to just the right book, just the right place at just the right time, or just the right person. It is as if we have an Internal Self-Help Barometer that guides us more perfectly as we reach each new increment of our willingness to pay attention.

The books, places, situations, and people we are drawn to when we follow this Barometer will mysteriously offer the answer to a pressing question or somehow lead us on to the next step of our inner journey to Wholeness. I'm sure you've experienced this before. It happens all the time!

This does not, however, mean that the answer is outside us: We can take credit for trusting the feelings that led us into that right situation in the first place. The Truth has many ways of making Itself known, and since we are all One in Truth, the One uses us All to help each one of us find It.

Acknowledging this mystery, going with the flow, and going within, we can transform our thinking. This will transform our bodies, our circumstances, our lives. We can Glow With Inner Beauty and be healers to all around us.

Glow With Inner Beauty? you ask sarcastically, adding, *How can I Glow With Inner Beauty while I still feel as though I Reel From Self-Abuse?*

AWAKEN
IN THE LIGHT

IDEAS
ON HOW
ONE GOES ABOUT
AWAKENING IN THE LIGHT

Imagine yourself as a Being of Light.
Notice how it feels to Become Light.

Imagine that every particle and atom in
your body is saturated with tingly,
refreshing, renewing Light.

Focus on the Source of Light within yourself.
Where is it? Where does it comes from?
Practice generating Light.

See the world bathed in just the right amount
of your Love and Light. What does that feel like?
What is meant by just the right amount?

Close your eyes, and with your inner vision or
inner feeling, notice what Colors of Light
are in different parts of your body.

Practice bringing in The Light in a busy
supermarket line where everyone seems
impatient and unhappy to be there.
Notice what happens.

Aren't you changing the subject? Weren't we just talking about all the terrible things I do? All my addictions and habits? How can I jump from the middle of my worst flaws right into the Shining Light?

WE CAN FEEL THE LIGHT WITHIN. Imagine it starting as a seed, a speck, in the Center of your being. That Center is vast, unlimited.

Come on, now, you're not even going to answer my question?

Let the light grow and spread through you until every cell in your body is tingling with it, until every cell in your body overflows with it, creating a radiant aura, giving life and love to the world. How does this feel?

This is ridiculous. I'm not supposed to feel all tingly.

Bringing our attention back to the speck in the Center, we can allow it to unfold and overflow again, this time feeling the light on an even deeper cellular level.

Go for it, gently now, F l o w   L i g h t   G r o w   M o v e   U n i t e ...

Whoa.

Allowing the healing light to grow and spread within is a form of nourishment, a kind of food. When we take time out to nourish ourselves in this way, we have more to give—in all our relationships and to ourselves.

We may find we feel more relaxed, and that some of the mental anxiety and torment that used to be so all-pervasive may seem to have been...washed away. Our every action can speak of quality and care, good timing, and right thinking.

What is The Light? We can ask ourselves.

Well that felt really good, I'll admit. But, what would everybody think of me if I went around talking about The Light?

WHAT OTHERS THINK OF ME IS NONE OF MY BUSINESS

IDEAS TO MAKE
WHAT OTHERS THINK OF US
BECOME NONE OF OUR BUSINESS

*When tempted to,
don't ask another's opinion.*

*Next time you feel that someone is
criticizing you or putting you down in
word or in thought, ignore it. Bite your tongue.
Do not agree or respond, in thought or deed.*

Listen to another's idea; then Do It Your Own Way.

*Pretend that you can create a force field around
yourself which emanates from that central spark of
Light. Imagine that only loving, positive,
nurturing thoughts from others can penetrate it.*

*See the Inner Light in someone who is speaking about
you in anything less than the most cheerful, pleasant
and helpful manner, while s/he is doing it.*

*Create or borrow a Personal Power Affirmation to say
to yourself any time you have a negative thought.
(You'll find a few in this chapter.)*

Spend some quiet time alone, instead of going out.

WE HAVE BEEN CONDITIONED TO SEEK APPROVAL FROM OUTSIDE SOURCES. The idea of our wrongness goes deep, but now we can heal it.

As we realize Who We Are, the illusion of need for approval fades away. Whether others are so-called right or so-called wrong is irrelevant. What matters is our personal integrity and faith in our own ability to take care of ourselves. We can answer our own questions, solve our own problems! We can trust ourselves.

Do you realize how exciting this is?

While this concept is new to us, we may need to protect ourselves from the toxic thoughts of others. Even though we are changing, even though we got so sick of living the old way and of being in pain all the time, others may not be ready to heal. This does not mean we need to judge them or criticize them or think we are superior. They have been criticized and have been in pain, just as we have, and they will change when they want to.

It may mean, however, that we will want to put a little fence of protection around ourselves, like we would for a young sapling. We will begin to be aware of how negative thoughts feel when others project them.

Wait, hold it.

First, you want me to Become Light. Now you want me to Feel Thoughts? Isn't that a little too New-Agey?

Actually we do it all the time. We just may not realize we are doing it. Haven't you ever walked into a room feeling fine, only to realize a moment later that you are crossing your hands over your chest, that you feel a funny sensation in your solar plexus, that something just doesn't *feel* right? Out of confusion and because we are used to feeling like we are the bad guy, we may have thought these sensations were another signal that something's wrong with us. But that's not true. We are feeling thoughts.

We can begin to choose not to *react* to these thoughts. If we react to them out of our old mental habits, we would probably end up beating up on ourselves mentally again. Understanding that these thoughts could hurt us if we let them, perhaps we will decide to end or alter certain unhealthy relationships, or to leave places when we get those funny feelings. Whoever said we had to stay there? Whoever said we had to accept those thoughts?

When we become fully aware that negative thoughts projected from others hurt us, we are open to a major realization: our

our negative thoughts hurt others, too. This is a biggie, a painful one to look at. And getting it, understanding its implications, can literally change our life. Take a moment to just think about this.

ॐ

Feeling and owning this in the middle of our being will empower us to curb our tendency to mentally bash others, however innocent that bashing may seem. Remember when you were driving to work and someone pulled out in front of you and you called that driver something particularly unfriendly in your mind or out loud? Didn't you feel a struggle, a slight battle going on between you? Who was the victor? Who really lost?

The point is, we have all accumulated a veritable toxic waste dump in the mind, and others unwittingly become natural dumping grounds for all this garbage because we don't know what else to do with it.

We are all in it together, so there is no need to blame or make the situation worse by feeling guilty about it. What is helpful is to *notice* when we do it and replace the thought of attack with a thought of blessing, remembering that we are ALL Children of Love. Try creating an affirmation to repeat often, such as, "I Live In The Light Of Life," or "All Is Well In My World," or "Bless That Man Who Just Pulled Out In Front Of Me."

If you think this sounds too corny, you never have to tell anyone about it. It can be your secret. Anytime you find yourself thinking a negative thought about yourself or someone else, or about any situation you may find yourself in, just replace it with your Personal Power Affirmation or with one spontaneously created to suit the present situation. And never, never give up on yourself!

Hey—you...you tricked me! We started this chapter talking about how others have been so mean and have had such bad thoughts about me, and you switched it to make me aware of the fact that I have a part in creating and maintaining all this ugliness. You mean you want me to admit stuff like that?

Yes. What we put out comes back to us. Not Harming others, we are Not Harmed. Healing ourselves, we heal the world. Forgiving ourselves, we open to the possibility of forgiving the world.

This is deep.

This is true self love.

I
LOVE
MYSELF

TECHNIQUES FOR REMEMBERING THAT YOU LOVE YOURSELF

Do something kind for yourself.
Buy yourself flowers, maybe, and put
them with water in a lovely vase or
an empty spaghetti-sauce jar.

Look at your reflection in the mirror
and send love to yourself through your eyes.
Allow the good feelings to well up inside.

When you feel like crying,
notice if it feels safe to do this.
If so, even if it's a little scary,
allow yourself the cleansing tears.

Do something kind for someone else.
Be spontaneous.

Imagine what it would be like
if everyone on earth felt love for all of
creation at the same moment.

WHAT DOES IT MEAN TO LOVE ONE'S SELF? The ancient chivalrous knights believed that Love is Perfect Kindness. When we have kindled the kindness within, we then have that kindness to give others.

I see. Before, all I had to give was all the meanness and bad thoughts and criticisms I had stored so unhappily for all this time—even though I wasn't completely terrible, and I did have good thoughts once in a while. But now, I can begin to fill myself with something a little more pleasant, on purpose.

Exactly.

One of the present goals of humanity is to come together in peace. It is hard work, struggling along as we have been, doing things that harm us and harm those around us. One thing holding us in that rut is Self-Pity.

Let me explain and re-cap. Self-Pity is a mechanism we use to keep ourselves in despair. Staying in a state of despair seems comfortable because we are used to it. We are used to it because this is what we have been taught, by those to whom it has been taught. This may feel like a hovering, pervasive, undefinable sense of uneasiness and lack. It's kind of like being stuck in the middle of a dark cloud, with faint memories of sunny

~

days; you long for the sun, but you're not sure it really exists.

To say, "It is easy to overcome this illusionary form of self-deprivation," is both true and untrue:

In the Ultimate Reality, yes—it is easy! Every moment holds the key; every millisecond contains the potential for us to open our hearts to the Source, to the tingly excitement of Life, to the renewing forces of Bliss.

It is also difficult because we have been so thoroughly conditioned away from this peace and self-love. We have come to feel sorry for ourselves and to think we cannot have what is pure and what is good.

Therefore, it is both easy and difficult. And when we can fully embrace this paradox—allowing ourselves to experience the challenge of overcoming our conditioning through dedicated action, while allowing ourselves the possibility of moments of Pure Experience where ALL pain is washed clean, where ALL mistakes are forgiven, where nothing exists but the Deepest Peace—then, we align ourselves fully with our unique, individual healing path.

ॐ

The earth is a land of paradox, where stillness meets the noisy sea. The tree embraces earth, and heaven, too. As we walk this world of opposites, let's crest the wave of bliss, then ride the calmest emptiness, to hear within the Everlasting Truth.

Is this what you mean?

Yes...my, my...you're getting it!

I HAVE MY OWN PATH, AND IT IS BEAUTIFUL

IDEAS FOR
STEPPING BEAUTIFULLY
ONTO YOUR OWN PATH

*When something
"bad" happens, ask,
"What can I learn from this?
How can I become stronger? What is
this person or situation trying to teach me?"*

*Drive or walk to work a different way
than usual, following your feelings.*

*Relax and visualize walking on
Your Inner Path. Notice what it
looks and feels and smells
and sounds like.
What is behind you?
What is in front of you?*

*Make a list of
all the things you love to do,
and figure out how often you allow yourself
to do them. Is there an adjustment
you'd like to make in the do
to not-do ratio?*

ACCEPTING THE CHALLENGE TO GROW BEYOND OUR PAST CONDITIONING IS AN ACT OF RESPONSIBILITY. Part of that conditioning has been to give our power away to others. When we were children, our parents seemed All-Powerful. Though they were doing the best they could at the time—they really were—we may have emerged from that relationship feeling, well, less than fully empowered. This lack of self-empowerment may have caused us to seek jobs where we felt dependent, or relationships where we struggled for control.

Nevertheless, we now have the power to choose something different. Let me mention something scary:

We are all totally responsible—100% responsible—for all of our actions, for all of our thoughts, for our own Path, for our own Life, for everything that happens to us in life. We are not victims. We are *not* victims.

Ugghh.

I thought you might say that. But now that you've heard the worst, here's the payoff, which makes the worst sound not so bad after all:

Accepting that response-ability, we free ourselves from bondage to blame and disempowerment. We no longer give our power away by saying, "They did it to me." We claim our unique ability to be the Master Of Our Own Life! Self-responsibility frees us completely from outside authority.

Oh! Hmmm...

Of course, practicing this concept may mean anything from owning your ability to create your life the way you want it to be, to leaving a note on the windshield of a Mercedes-Benz whose tail light you accidentally busted out. Here are some affirmations that may help, or you could make up one of your own:

I NOW CHOOSE SELF-RESPONSIBILITY.

I HONOR MY ABILITY TO TAKE CARE OF MYSELF.

**I AM A POWERFUL, CAPABLE BEING
OF LOVE AND LIGHT.**

**I NOW CLAIM MY SACRED ABILITY TO RESPOND
IN PERFECT WAYS TO ALL OF LIFE'S SITUATIONS.**

**USING MY ABILITY TO RESPOND IN PERFECT WAYS,
I MANIFEST HARMONY & ABUNDANCE
IN ALL AREAS OF MY LIFE.**

In my case, it wasn't actually a busted tail light or a Mercedes Benz, but I tell you, the car owners were pleasantly surprised that someone actually owned up to the error, and in two situations, I ended up having to pay for nothing, even though I was fully willing to pay for it all. This idea of taking resonsibility may seem scary... it may seem like the price we'd pay would be too high.

But just try it. You may find that, in fact, it is magic! You may find that it is a crucial step on your Path and that a chance to test the concept may arrive sooner than you think! (You'll know when it happens. You'll feel the overwhelming urge to ask, *Do I really have to do this?* Just take a deep breath. It'll be okay.)

(6)

The journey to self-responsibility is a deep inner quest, because we must confront and move through many of the fears that have kept us in shackles. But all will be well. *No matter what happens all will be well* because we will KNOW that we are in the process of growing into the fullness of our own power, which we find gently residing in our innermost being.

I see; let me see if I can explain: Honoring the deep truths we find on our inner journeys, we can each walk our OWN path in per-

fect love and perfect trust, accepting 100% responsibility for our own lives. Following the flow of life within us, we honor our bodies, each other, the earth and all her plants, rocks, places, and creatures, and our Truest Self—Life, Love, Light.

Yeah. You're good! And now, looking beyond all words to their deeper meaning within us, we learn again to Walk In Beauty.

PART TWO

✳

The path to wholeness

is one wrought with care by God-In-Us.

Along the way, we need not be angry at the shadows.

BEAUTY WITHIN ME, BEAUTY ALL AROUND ME, IN BEAUTY I WALK

IDEAS
ON HOW TO
WALK IN BEAUTY

*Notice the Inner Beauty
of another being. Notice how
you feel when you do this.*

*What would it be like if you gave a real,
heart-warming, genuine smile to
the next person you saw?*

*Take an unhurried,
unstructured walk and
stop to pet the cats, smile at the
children, touch, smell and appreciate the plants and
flowers, and hug the trees.* (Hold on. Did you say, "hug
the trees"? *Yes. Remember the chapter that starts,
"What Other People Think of Me...?")*

*How does it feel in your heart, to hug
a tree? (You can do it when no
one is looking, at first,
if you like.)*

*Notice how nature
works in circles.
Feel what a
circle is.*

MANY NATIVE AMERICANS SPEAK OF LIVING THE BEAUTY WAY — living each day in harmony with all our fellow beings on the planet, including plants, animals, insects, birds, trees, rocks, and other humans. What does it mean to live in harmony?

I think harmony springs from appreciating our everyday relationships and the gifts of the natural world. Can you imagine what the earth would be like without the peace of a river flowing gently through a forest, or the majesty and cold peaks of mountains? Think about it. We decorate our homes with floral wall paper, fake plants or real plants, photographs of sunsets, pictures of ducks on lakes. Some people go fishing or play golf or prune the bushes just for an excuse to be outside!

NATURE is what we want. We want the peace of clean crisp air, we long for a refreshing day off at the beach. We work so hard every day just to earn a little piece of outdoor recreation and relaxation. Many times, though, we become too harried and tired to desire anything but sleep when we finally have a day off, if we have one at all, between shopping, family and other activities.

Maybe our working days wouldn't be so hard if we would just walk outside and appreciate the tree in the parking lot. Or stop from our work and glance up into the sky, noticing that a cloud looks like our favorite childhood dog running up to greet us. Or take a deep breath of fresh air after momentarily poking our head out the door, smiling when we hear a little bird singing his song. What is this bird trying to say?

These simple practices give us energy, literally. Just try it. Come on, it'll be fun! Get up now, go outside, and take a deep breath. Pause. Just stand there a moment, breathing. How do you feel? How much better do you feel?

When we have more energy through this kind of relaxation and breathing and connection with nature, we can begin to take ourselves to the next level of our Quest. Just trust yourself. You may find that you want to move in a certain way outdoors, maybe in a dance-like fashion. Why not try it? It will feel really good. Maybe you'll be inspired to run or to gently exercise, in a natural way, not forced, in balance with your own energy, in a way that will GIVE you more energy.

Going outside and sitting down on the ground is an amazingly helpful thing to do when emotionally upset. Though we all reach higher levels of inner peace on our journey to Wholeness, there may be days when we feel stuck again, feeling sad or angry. Or that overriding unhappiness may sneak in again unwanted.

So consider sitting on the ground. Reconnecting with the balancing forces of the earth allows us to sort through our feelings. We may find asking questions to be helpful. "What is this upset teaching me? Is there something I need to change about the way my life is going? Is there anything I feel thankful for? Is there someone I am having trouble understanding? What is this person trying to teach me? Where does my relationship to The Source fit into this whole scenario? Is the Source Of All really paying any attention to me or interested in me?"

The answers, you will find, flow to you naturally, just as you ask them. You will *know.*

I
KNOW
THE WAY

IDEAS
FOR TAPPING
YOUR KNOWING

*Think about
anything you
know to be true.
Notice how you feel in
your body when you think of it.*

*Notice when the words
of another make you question
your own knowing. How does this feel?*

*Figure out how to get back to your inner
knowing after self-doubt
has slipped in.*

WITH ALL THE DISTRACTIONS OF MODERN LIFE, PART OF US HAS FORGOTTEN THAT WE KNOW. It just takes a little bit of slowing down to reattune ourselves to our knowing. A few quiet moments each day with NO distractions is a good way to start. This will joyfully grow into a life-enhancing habit of creating spaces of deep peace in our lives because it feels so good!

It is possible to change. It is possible to heal. This we KNOW deep within.

The Choice is ours.

We must really apply this concept. We must actually get quiet, by ourselves, close our physical eyes, open our internal eyes, and SEE.

(Don't be surprised if you start to feel all tingly.)

There are hundreds of published and taught techniques for doing this. Many of these may be helpful to you. Trust your gut instinct implicitly when it comes to these things.

My belief is that you already know how to do it and that if you actually sit down and make an effort to go deep into the silence, you will succeed. My challenge to you is to try it. Then you will own it.

Thinking about it and talking about it and doing it haphazardly with no real focus will not bring great results. You've got to want it. You've got to want it for the right reasons—for Love, for healing, for the desire toward Connection to All Things. We must Re-Member our Connection. We must Eat our truth and Digest it fully. We do this in the inner silence.

open to the
Mouth of God
speak within,
and empty

open to the
Mouth of God
speak within,
and empty

open to the
Mouth of God
speak within,
and empty

RETURN TO CENTER, THAT ADDRESS NOW KNOWN!

IDEAS FOR ASSISTING YOURSELF IN YOUR RETURN TO CENTER

*Make a
circle on the floor
with rocks or something
and sit in the
middle of it.*

*Figure out what
it feels like and means
to be "grounded."*

*Find the center
of your body. Draw
the breath there.*

*Lie down
on the floor and
deeply relax.*

*Decide
how committed
you are to your
Own Path.*

WHERE IS THE CENTER? What is it? What does it feel like? Is it beyond ordinary perception? Does it have a location in time and space, in the body? Is it everywhere at the same time?

What does this mean, everywhere at the same time? Is it in me? Is it you? Does it emanate from within the old man who asked for a dollar the other day? How do we *know?* How do we *Get There?* There... there... feel it? *Remember?*

There is nothing to say
once I reach You,
no words to find me
once I am there.
Albeit the silence is Something,
there is nothing to say,
there is nothing to—
there is...

I want to share something very important with you. You are a Divine Being, complete unto Yourself. Your gift, the True Thing You Have Come Here To Do, is so important that Creator Within brought you forth just to do it! In manifest form, you embody a Divine Idea. You are here to serve and help mankind in your own unique way, and to learn and grow, and to return to knowledge of your Oneness With All Things, your Sacred Essential Essence, your love of God—whatever you wish to call God, the One Life, the All.

Back in the depths of our beginnings, we may have been aware of this purpose, this evolutionary ideal that we each carry as a seed within us.

When you stepped into the clothing of a human form, with all the other people's thoughts and agendas about who you were, you may have temporarily forgotten that Essence of yourself. Temporarily.

You see, all the little messages and hints and undeniable feelings that *there is something more to life and you are a part of it* are true.

Welcome, Joyous One! Welcome into the Circle of Life, where You reside in Purity and Perfection. Welcome into the Center, Your Center. All of Creation welcomes your birth into the Knowledge of Who You Are, deep within, all around. All of Creation is waiting with bated breath, and the Sureness of God's Love, for you to rediscover your purpose, your meaning, your evolutionary ideal—the very Gift you came here to give!

Believe it or not, Your Unique Gift is *essential* to—part of the *essence* of—the Evolution of Mankind. Yes. Just let that sink in for a moment. Can you grasp this? Can you really get it?

To fully realize and grasp and own this is a truly Amazing Experience. I'm not joking. Can you imagine what it feels like to wake up one day (literally or figuratively) and say, *I Am a Part of ALL Things!? My existence Is. I Am Blessed and Loved and Loving, I Am Love Itself! And I have Something to offer, Something to do that no one else can do!* Just pretend you can imagine this possibility. Suspend disbelief for just one second....

You may think this all sounds corny. That's ok. Because even if it sounds corny, even if you can't imagine being *that* essential and loved, a little part of you may be saying, thank goodness, thank goodness, it is true.

AFTER WORDS

*

Witness here the mighty roar,
deep within the Womb of time

of timelessness that never ends,

beckoning

to reckon with the One within.

The trumpets cease
and Still begins to quiver into Silence.

The One Within is Silence ever pressing.

IDEAS
ON WHAT IN
THE WORLD TO
DO WITH YOURSELF
AFTER READING
THIS BOOK

*Take
a bath.*

*Go to work,
go to the store.*

*Go to bed, get up
in the morning,
brush your teeth.*

*And, most importantly,
Pay Attention.*

THIS BOOK HAS BEEN FILLED WITH IDEAS YOU MAY FIND HELPFUL ON YOUR JOURNEY TO THE CENTER. The truth is, you do know the way, and your path will unfold with greater and greater clarity each day if you want it to. I can tell you that I have asked for healing, and I have received it. I have asked for Peace, and it has danced gently into my heart, springing into a fullness I never dared dream possible! If it can be so with me, it can be so with you. We are all connected in the One Life.

For me, the healing has times of clarity and times of wading through the thick stuff of misunderstanding and outworn neural patterning. We need not judge the process; we need not judge ourselves when we are "in the thick of it."

We may, however, want to acknowledge our willingness to dive into the thick of it in the first place as the Act of Pure Bravery that it is! And we will succeed. There is a long, brilliant line of Light behind us, within us, and paving the way forward into a Bright Future for Mankind and Planet Earth. *Yes! Aho! So Be It!*

We ride an Eternal Wave on our Endless Journey, and the key element is Trust. When we reach a peak in our transformative work, it is as if we have conquered great heights. We are standing at the mountain's summit, breathing crisp air, absorbing—being—the crystalline Light.

We deserve the deep fulfillment, the Completion. And as we shift our golden vision to witness Beauty around us—ah! What grander peaks are those? Unhesitatingly, in the Spirit of Pure Adventure, we start afresh. What an immensely challenging, rich, and fun thing it is to live!

Peace be with you.
May the Light within you
show forth in abundant measure,
as beacon and blessing to the world.
May each of your days be blessed.
May all your Perfect Dreams come True!

So be it!

AWAKE!
INCORPORATED

BE ON THE
LOOKOUT:
MORE TOOLS FOR
SELF-READJUSTMENT
IN THE LIGHT COMING
TO YOU SOON!

Check out
Laura's Web Site:
creativespirit.home.mindspring.com

LAURA CRUGER FOX
CREATIVE SPIRIT
(804) 355-7567
Available Through New Leaf
& by special order through Ingram

BRIGHTEST
BLESSINGS!